Water's Leaves & Other Poems

Water's Leaves & Other Poems
GEOFFREY NUTTER

Winner of the 2004 Verse Prize

Verse Press Amherst, Massachusetts

Acknowledgments

I would like to thank the publications in which some of these poems first appeared: *Carnet de Route, Chicago Review, Colorado Review, Euphony, Hayden's Ferry Review, jubilat, Verse, Xantippe,* and *The Iowa Anthology of New American Poetries.*

Thanks to the Museum of Modern Art for commissioning "Boy Leading a Horse."

Thanks also to Nick Rockwell, and to David Joel Friedman.

Published by Verse Press

Verse Press titles are distributed to the trade by Consortium Book Sales and Distribution, 1045 Westgate Drive, St. Paul, Minnesota 55114.

Library of Congress Cataloging-in-Publication Data:

Nutter, Geoffrey, 1968-
  Water's leaves & other poems / Geoffrey Nutter.-- 1st ed.
    p. cm.
  ISBN-13: 978-0-9746353-6-1 (pbk. : alk. paper)
  ISBN-10: 0-9746353-6-7 (pbk. : alk. paper)
  I. Title: Water's leaves and other poems. II. Title.
  PS3614.U88W38 2005
  811'.6--dc22
                         2005007249

Design, composition and cover photograph by J. Johnson.
Author photograph by Paul DeSilva.

Printed in the United States of America

9 8 7 6 5 4 3 2 1

First Edition

Contents

The Experiment

We were waiting in a windowless room.
But we had our imagination
which we sharpened like reeds and grasses
and gathered together like a quiver
of feather-light arrows. The experiment
began abruptly
with a phrase, with a signal,
with a weight slowly lowered
through white steam. And the phrase
might have been about the sale
of trees and sunken boats, and the
signal was the arc
of a bright green arrow. And daylight
is crossing the footbridge.
What are we waiting for?
A green-yellow
marksman. A whisper through
a fine mesh. Raindrops
boiling in a silver kettle.
Daylight is crossing the footbridge.
Daylight is crossing the footbridge
that leads into a dark city, and crossing
the strong light of grasses darkening cities.
We see ourselves crossing it, though we are here.
We have released ourselves like arrows
into the sunlight.

Journey by Train

We are better than nature. We are better than ourselves.
We emerged from the tunnel, the sun was dazzling,
it blinded us, all was light-whiteness, until our train
passed behind the stadium.

Then we were on the lanes. Gamine as cats, beautiful
in leopard robes and tangible, huge as epipsychidion.
The streetlamps were popping on like miracles as the
sky darkened. Light glowed in the tips of silver quills—
spring stars, all a-glory without us. Were terrible, were
vogue as new suns, were the skeptical waters of the rain.

We are the smallest, the weakest, the poorest, the
frailest; we are victory. Least loveable, least worthy,
least beautiful, above the black steeples, the rooftops,
the water towers cut in crocodilian figures in the sky;
blackened by smoke in appearance, by smog, by dirt; we
emerge into the forest after rain, I bring you, tall, dark,
and thin, a shy girl in the whimsical trees.

The Definition of Swan

One that resembles or emulates a swan
may be rightly called a "Swan," or more precisely,
"one who emulates a swan." We may say that he is swan-like.
If he is long-necked and beautiful, or if he flies strongly
when once started, or sleeps in mim,
we may put him to sleep in a swannery.
To "swan" is to wander aimlessly.
Clouds become claws and cover the sun.
An emu on the riverbank is lucent, supervenes.
She eyes the octagons unfolding in the rushes
and finds, when they've unfolded,
the strange eight known as "Swan."
There now. Do they migrate?
Who knows. They float, detached, like constellations,
or a man who pedals passengers along the banks
in a large model of a swan.
Something happens: a woman executes a dive
with her head back, back arched,
and her arms spread sideways, then brings them together
to form a straight line
with her body as she enters the water;
this is called a "swan-dive."
But doesn't it look something like a prayer,
or a way to make love?
It may resemble both, as the clouds resemble crows,
or mountains, or mist in the mountains, or mist minus
mountains, or all of the above.
I wish her name was Cygnus.

Trees Choosing a King

Let us dip our hand into the Stream
of Temptation, that we might know
and be merciful. For we can hear
the noise of cataracts somewhere
in the distance, its whispering,
its whispering the parable
of the Trees Choosing a King.
And we can walk along the banks
toward the edge of the sea where the wind
is handling chestnuts in branches,
and the house where the trellised jasmine
breaks the sun into shadows
that flicker on the childbed in a bare room.
These things are common as grass.

Milagros Cordero

We're passing the whole summer, all of us,
in the country, in a field, where we sleep
under the stars in one another's arms,
with wet grass printing patterns on our hands
where we lean back or fall back into the grass
to sleep under the stars.

It's beautiful to be,
and to be outside where the wind is, with the friends
who love you most all summer under stars. And Mary
is there, and another girl too, and so is Milagros Cordero,
and at this moment I'm running toward the others
hand in hand with them, and they're laughing
and Maria turns to kiss me in front
of a circle or a sickle shape of friends
reclining on the earth to show that all is well
and that we are ourselves but not quite ourselves.
We have abandoned ourselves completely
to be completely with each other,
if only for a few moments, to have our only
moment in the sun and be as grass,
green and instantaneous.

Why don't I live
this way, where the great yellow disc harrow
lies rusting in the wildly overflowing grass,
and high gazing trees that taper into green points
incline a little in the sky, where they are living
always with the wind, a magnificent thing, and all
that is beloved is evergreen.

Listen: there has been
a great storm. Massive clouds have passed before us,
and passed in front of the sun, and darkened

gray-green bridges. We were wading ankle-deep
by sloping green faucets, dark gentlemen were watching
from the windows of a topaz structure,
and air balloons drifted over the heartless craters, tilting
toward Stara Zagora.
                          How were we brought
through the storm like conquerors, made transparent
like petals in the rain, somehow set down gently here?
We awaken under rain-green flags, alive
for a single day.

Century Morning

The tube of red paint leaking on the Redband,
the backsliding egret a-wing on a bucolic century,
forgotten like Parnassus in the Fragonard, its
peak a gray gaffe, a gray man in oilcloth;
Under the sensor eye above the door of the Check Cashing
Pavilion, in the gray rain's quintillions, a door
slides open almost noiselessly—it is the sound
of a century beginning. It is the gentle wish
to be silent and untouchable—shhh. Shoo fly.
The window is open, the high window,
it has always been open and it is a long way down
to the pear orchard's wet palaver and the morning dew.
Let's call it a day. Let's call it what we have longed for
but never named: The sum of our desires.

Invitation

The scheme to be evil all day in the solemn
grass had its flaws. Now you are upset and you
are wondering what to do. Your plans were finely
laid; it was a full-fledged project. Paper-
clips and staples sing in high sopranos.
You were nightfowling at the gates
of Rushvan, rousing birds from sleep
with a bell, dazzling them with light
and collecting them into snares.

Where is the small part of the world you had
on the day you were born? Before you awoke
to the sound of waves, a basket of fire,
a bird, a snow-white thing, a bell.
I woke up mother-naked in the sand.
And the blue-green sea was in front of me
like glittering terracotta bands on the side
of a blue-green building, where machines
were shredding beautiful archives.

Who stood there clear as rain, feet in the
surf, ice in his beard, raising an ancient ceramic
hand? His demands are remorseless. His
is the withering rhetoric abounding
with a bold and meaningless number centered
on every page, on every leaf. It is the stuff
of distances. His is the kettle of boiling
raindrops. It is the double-cross of the
beloved.

The Black Dog

When I was walking in the woods
with a gun and a great and undulating V
of ducks above me and the red

leaves of the maples sweet and crystallized
I saw a black dog come out of a pond
and break into a million light-tipped crystals

as he shook the water from his fur.
I was Distorted Man—distorted by what
I did not know. And what Avatar

came sparkling then? And what
spark-bedizened wand came shooting
off sparks and formed the Sparkling

Man? I was Blinded Man—blinded by
a great distorting thing. The black
dog came and licked my hand.

Sí, the Nevid Fruit

A black bird with an orange beak
sits in a black cube. Some kid
did this to be funny—but it's not.

This same kid saw lilacs sprouting
in a forest of twisting horns.
"It's just so liquid cosmic, okay?"
he said, laughing nervously.
"It almost makes me forget about..."

It made him forget about kissing her,
whose hair was big green leaves.
And taking a drink from a glass
of clear, cold berry-nut juice.

He split the fruit open to find
its jelly alive and touched
by nightfall.

Afternoon in Iceland

This was the book that slipped from your hands
when you nodded off to sleep: It was cold
outside like a bowl of red grapes. It was
unnervingly alive and wanting to stay alive.

A girl rode her bicycle over a bridge
in a city in Iceland on a cloudy day.
A few other people were crossing the bridge,
and a few plants dangled from the glass ceiling
where the sun was practicing her tuba.
A young man turns the blue and yellow faces
of a Rubik's Cube eternally.
Will he knuckle under to its vast superiority
of combinations? A man reading in a tea shop
drinking Arctic tea and jasmine sharpened
by an Arctic spring, open up the clouds,
the Book of Helmets, Book of Clouds,
a few white buildings stood in the clouds.

                    From your bed
and through the open window
you saw the white flags and the tall antennae
of the brown audio/visual building and apartments;
signposts stuck up through the broken foliage,
and later, a few snowflakes drifting down formally
like pages from a book of jurisprudence.

Wind turned the foxed pages of the book beside you:

There is a vital energy at loose in the world,
severe as an archaic helmet in the sun.

Years from now, when all sides of a colored cube
are suddenly aligned, every face will wear
its primary color, or an ice cube,
wear its color like a flag snapping in a near gale
on a cold, bright day on a bridge in an Icelandic city.

So it is not necessary for you to know
what we do here, or what function
you serve. You have been eating oranges
your whole life long without seeing
the tree. These are not for the eyes, this cold
smoke drifting past high windows,
the spruce rib-works of buildings
white and glassy in the sky.
What would require years of winter
for the wind to pick clean
seems to have been born that way,
mother-naked, in an instant.
The water-towers seem
to know something basic that you
have forgotten: They stand unsmiling
like children in a nineteenth-century
photograph who await the coming
of a great light.

Long have you kept your archives in this room,
in a sea-green filing cabinet, blond in the bristles
of a hairbrush. Go out from this small room
and tell me what is there, aside from red pods
on the white snow, and white birds
on the red snow; aside from blue-green terracotta
tiles on the sides of shimmering aqua buildings.
Aside from a nightgown floating through the chilly air.
It seems so strange that there
are no faces watching from those

blue-green rooms, where there are
red December flowers in blue-green
bowls, and people speaking other
languages, where lives that you
will never know are moving elegantly,
and life is flowing around you
like a cool evening breeze.
It is touching you serenely.

Look at the fragile red pinnacles
in front of the sunset: It appears that the whole
world is momentarily in love with you,
and repeats your name which you have chanted
dismally until this, a Sunday afternoon
with elegant sunlight dabbed
on lichen-covered stones.

The Wedding Gift

I was just thinking that thought.
How the Polish foundry city Ruda Śląska
woke to sun on the rubber cement.
Like a droplet of dew on an ear of maize:
the city shone.

You must have been thinking this too.
You, a man in the year 1211, just awake
from a dream where you carried a basket
of apples to a wedding feast.
With your boots in limewater and oarweed,
then your boots were somehow gone,
so you sloshed barefoot through the oarweed
as a storm came near, and nearer.
And we took refuge from the storm in a library
floating on the marsh, as the terrible thing
went on outside. And we could hear
the pan-pipes and the pine-pipes, and
could hear the syrinx in the treetops.

And then our thoughts coincided:
and the sun sheared off the tops of black tables,
leaving legs like columns that rose to the clouds
and the dark clouds were powerless
and the sorrowful avenged.
We saw the same thing, like a droplet
of dew, and we felt
the sun on our backs as we strode
arm in arm to the wedding.

The Peacock

Who is the setting sun with whom
the moon is in love? Who came
at seed-time in her flowered robes
taking the whole world by surprise,
coming through the semi-dark into a light
like nothing we had ever seen? An indelible
word made visible. The blue, illuminated page
of the roman à clef that guides him through
the folktale; he has curbed his strength,
belittled his might, as the dawn
fans out across the morning sky,
as the huge plumes of a peacock fast unfolding.

Flower Sermon

The monumental city
at the beginning of September:
it is the end of something.
A gleaming tripod
quick with energy tips
and is kicked over.
It is the end of a grammar
the child learned
in a school grown over with grass;
and the animals thriving
in the grass teach us something
else: the Flower Sermon,
smoke rising mild
and blue above the hickory.
I was a guest among
others; so were you.
I was frozen like a monument
under the sky; you
were too, but only
for an instant, like a building
inside of which many
had been schooled
but now lies open and bare
in the grass, listening.

The Paragon

Over by the estuary
there are windharps
hanging in the yellow
eucalyptus boughs.
There is a bucket and a spool
of thread, and a rainsluice
leading to the reservoir.
Fumes blow over the simmering
grass from the giant estuary
yachts.
But there is room
as well for us to imagine
wisteria, and blossoms
of wisteria. There is, in fact,
room for more than we
had thought—the sails crowd not
the sky, nor overwhelm the grass
and golden thread.
The engines and the rain
are moving in the world alike—
there is, in fact, room for them all,
and room for a paragon of every one,
and for the worst of each—
of this I have no doubt.

Tea, Chairs, and Cormorants

1

The sky continued to peruse itself.
Tea was boiling on the stove.
Someone walked into the kitchen, said
"cormorant" just like that.
As if he'd never heard the word.
And suddenly it filled with them.

The bird-watchers notice something belabored
in his manner. Like a saint
surrounded by silence or wings.
We expand in someone's binoculars.

The sky said "cormorant" and just like that
it filled with them.
The storm was like a saint surrounded by itself.
All the sounds listened and tried
to memorize each and every other.

(A small mark on the page became
the "l" in "blemish."
As if he'd never heard the word
suddenly it filled with them.

2

In the Japanese garden, every leaf
that falls is a made leaf.
And every fall a made fall.
Shadows are wrung skillfully

through a confection of branches.
Spaces built into the trees fold
an origami light.
Arrangements are made to ensure the eye
sweeps from left to right. And rests.
And begins again.
Flowers are stationed evenly
and weave a fine apparel.
Everything is hostage to its purpose.)

3

Again, the sky was talkative with cormorants.
The tea was busily being prepared.
He supplanted the white space with birds
and made them fly in careful patterns.
A small mark in the sky
expands in their binoculars.

4

I intend to build a garden
with these five particular things.
Where even the stones relay a message back and forth.
And supplant
with these five particular things
the kitchen's scoured silence.
Nothing belaboring watcher or watched.
And the plants stranded in their purpose.
And the eye forced upon their flawlessness.

Tea
is boiling on the stove.
A chair is made for sitting, is chopped out
from a tree.
And pressed into a shape.
He walked into the kitchen and said "cormorant"
and, like a chair where bird-nests burst
from seams in the upholstery
it is filled with something.
Steam from the boiling tea.
A contrivance of shadow.
Sounds that memorize themselves.
Now he walks into this garden,
shambles of branch and method and the storm
surrounds him like a saint's shirt.
We expand in someone's binoculars.
Eyes sweep from left to right. And rest.
And begin again.
And turn to this panel of rice-paper wall.
The tea is brewed to the proper taste and color
and we drink.

Water's Leaves

1   *Absalom and Silas*

The blue junk sailed into the peaceful harbor.
And the sky above, in clouds, turned like a cement mixer.
Absalom the boat was tossed by waves.
There, among us, things found some frivolous bezug,
    some beauty.
There were two ambiguities going on at once.
For you it's just like ball lightning over the sea, isn't it?
Well, yes and no.
It's like some magical thing.

Silas, trouble-pointed, watched the waves,
and felt the strange pang inside him
where the sun touched, felt his many evasions
like light assisting the newly blind.
The will, which needs to will, had no effect
on the waves and the clouds.

2   *The Strange Place*

The boat motoring down the river
sent a huge spray behind it like a crystal
bird's spread plumage. "But is there no
pear-eaten dwelling place?" intoned the captain.
I'm awakened, in shock and tears, in a place
I don't belong, where I don't remember
falling asleep, and where the sound of the river
crashing over beige stones sounds far away.
There are the pears, and rustic grass churches,

where the night jasmine grows yellow-green—
and the water voices are becoming touchable
as the sun falls ice cold on the red lanes.

The Stony Silence of Grassy Fields

Let's say we built ourselves in effigy
using a murder of crows, and the vastness of the sky
drifting down in their shape into us.
The ground is made so true with the addition of the dying leaves,

using a murder of crows, and the vastness of the sky
for good measure. Over there, the clouds. Over here
the ground is made so true with the addition of the dying leaves.
I wrapped around everything she had for me right then, even
    the rain

for good measure. Over there, the clouds. Over here
the rain figuring into the scene we thought we'd captured.
I wrapped around everything she had for me right then, even
    the rain
that preached itself to us "like silver spiders,"

the rain figured into the scene we thought we'd captured.
Out of the left-over sounds of the day, the gravel
that preached itself to us "like silver spiders,"
we could build a statue to ourselves.

Out of the left-over sounds of the day, the gravel
of our private music could be sifted out, and
we could build a statue to ourselves
to shine as new-born jet-planes shine. Most

of our private music could be sifted out, and
as the oleanders adjust themselves around the first frost

to shine as new-born jet-planes shine, most
of what we call "seeing" is actually "believing."

As oleanders adjust themselves around the first frost
how much are we inflicting on the Autumn? How much
of what we call "seeing" is actually "believing?"
My shadow on the flagstones somehow dramatizing

how much we are inflicting on the Autumn. How much
we shriveled into what we wanted it to do for us,
my shadow on the flagstones somehow dramatizing
how we are the policemen of the lake and branches.

We shriveled into what we wanted it to do for us,
and a "Thrace of wind" plagued the trees and acknowledged
how we are the policemen of the lake and branches.
The engines are revving. Like dutiful mountains they sang

and a "Thrace of wind" plagued the trees and acknowledged
their ascension. A blue that seems ersatz is wondrous.
The engines are revving. Like dutiful mountains they sang
far into a sky that seemed to welcome

their ascension. A blue that seems ersatz is wondrous,
and the meadows arrayed like a brochure of meadows
far into a sky that seemed to welcome
our poltergeists. We awake with the suspicion we've been used,

and the meadows arrayed like a brochure of meadows
convince us we can stare into the sun for hours. We claim
our poltergeists. We awake with the suspicion we've been used,
feeling everything's desire to be ours. Our dreams

convince us we can stare into the sun for hours. We claim
the landscape scrolling past the window, charmed,

feeling everything's desire to be ours. Our dreams
make us innocent, who run in the ferrying light of helicopters,

the landscape scrolling past the window, charmed
until our teeth are broken in our mouths.
Make us innocent, who run in the ferrying light of helicopters,
Televise our shapes across the fields so we may rest

until our teeth are broken in our mouths
and statues of crows and engine noises dramatizing who we are
televise our shapes across the fields so we may rest.
Until we have the answer

and statues of crows and engine noises dramatizing who we are,
let's say we built ourselves in effigy
until we have the answer
drifting down in their shape into us.

Landscapes

1 Nomen Dubium

The study of the subject
moving through a landscape
in summer or winter plumage,
through a vast triangle of moving
parts; colossal nouns develop
on the dark horizon, lumped
and pointed forms, dark green
structures, murky amber windows.
To follow it, track it finally
to an open space where the brine
on the ridge of its back
grows crisp in the sun, and it
waits. Two Siamese fighting fish
in the sky are caught in a deadly embrace.

2

We must discuss the problem of analogy,
of the Gentle City, a city in the mist
below blue hills, the green valley,
the city walls, and the municipal waste
incinerated by fires outside the city.
The clouds are trailing
through the sky and past
the tops of buildings,
the brace-work of the great
silver bridge, the grizzled leaves
of the towering eucalyptus.
I pass through the open squares

like an ox, a water bison
trundling over red stones
or the fifth incarnation
of a sparrow. Where
are you hidden? I looked
for you there in the town,
in the alleys; shirts were drying
on glinting clotheslines in the sun.
The architecture of an ancient place
divided us—but could we have been thinking
a thought, we two, that nobody else
in the world was thinking?

3

A giant man strode forth upon the snows
of the sands in a white coat with collars
and wrote the prescription on a great yellow
pad in silver ink like light on the mythic
towers. There is snow half covering
the great yellow pad of the earth.

4 *Icy, Sky-Altering Stars*

Exultation kindled
within the ice water glass
to be so hit by sunshine.
She was amazed within herself
and the icy oblongs chucked
and clinked and chuckled.
The crystal chinks knocked
like battle-gear together,
no anguish, no blemish; just
such profit for the clean blue air,

just joyous iron javelins flying
over the snow of a desolate place,
and icy sky-altering stars.

That What Happen

The President said, "A tree grows here so strong
and so on top of me. It is dreamed by a man.
It is called a fish."
A girl with tangled hair came running
and poured magic ink on his pants.
He slept, and while she poured ink in his hair
he kept sleeping. Sleeping with blue ink
and small twigs in his hair
he kept dreaming. He dreamed he was a tree
and when he woke up he hypnotized the girl.
The girl became what he told her. The grass grew
and was the President.

When the man came back he said bye to the girl
and she slipped into the brook and was a fish.
"It's a dream," said the President.
He sat in the wind where the fish could see him.
The wind touched his back and rippled through him.
Where wind and rain worked so did the President.
He enacted his works.

He meant to make it seem small by calling it dream.
But the people worshipped the fish.
The fish levitated in the sea like glass.
The fish stopped dreaming they were the President
and hypnotized the people. All along the grassy beach
the people looked into the glass.
They couldn't reach the fish. They couldn't see the fish.
The fish levitated above them.

So there was a time of plenty.
A magic book was read to them aloud.

The President grew wild. In places it grew
tall enough for trees to hide in.
A girl ran through it.
She played on the green President.
She pursued her shadow through the President
until her shadow rose like wild hair.
She ran through its labyrinth of hedges
and couldn't reach the end of him.

In November, red leaves
adorned the President and covered him
all over: mulch, trimmings, leaves
rotting into the damp President.
The President soaked with rain.
In the morning, a shining, dew-soaked President,
lapels festooned with dandelions.

This is the most human-like
of the fish that levitate above them.
His eyes are blue and piercing.
If indeed we remove her from where she plays by the sea
she will perhaps become a brook, which will run beside him.
With his green tuxedo and wonderful hair
he will grow beside the brook.

Giant Water Bugs

I'm talking to giant water bugs...and they're built.
Yes, they're beautiful; yes, I'd marry them all if I could.
My moods change all the time.
I am a white car shooting a blue spotlight into the sky!
Then I am a small animal with wet hair, a cat with feathery wings.
You're beautiful, astonishing, unbelievable, amazing,
    hypnotic, terrific.
You're giant, enormous, bigger than a tree, of marvelous stature, a
towering, giant flowering bird!
What's that flaring out of the sun-rooted rigs?
A tree of great stature.
With what loveliness you loom with rapture over me.
There is nothing like you anywhere.

Ocean's Red Bio-Novel Nights

The sun settled gently like a lotus, covering the land.
It would be evening soon.
It is a city of canals, an image of a land
whose surfaces, blue liquid, brighten in the afternoon
to reflect a thousand buildings. See them then. Catch
them in the swoon
of their waking dream.
When she is walking, at night, a child notices the moon,
and it walks beside her. She sees it moving with her like
    a stream.
The night assists her. All things come to what they seem.

Hello smoke.
Did you see me roll, all alone down that hill and go
past the canals until my wheels broke, and birds broke
from the trees smudged along the sky, until we were far below
them. My teeth were aching when I saw them flow
as from a spigot, gently toward the mountain-tops
that dominate the summer day in winter snow,
three teeth, snow-domed and total, three giant drops
of platinum. A copse

originates mainly from shoots or root suckers rather than
    seed. Adown
in the red ground of the bordering dale
their roots were charmed like cobras from their lairs as
    the sun went down,
and their green hoods spread. A polygon of vale,
a cube of galingale,
and further off the city in her neon hair whose people
    and apologies appear the same,

like blades of grass. Sun, they pale in your sanitizing flame.
Still, they're glad you came.

I'm not much more than a stem
without roots, a thin thing. Something gave
me dreams. I arrived in a city, people told me things. I
    want to swallow them
whole, because I want them; I love, I have Love, but first
    I have desire.
Mostly desire. I wave,
like kelp, in the changing currents of that want. Dreams rave
inside the dreamer. Through the mist the sun was rising
    and exacting; so it spake
to Euclid of volition: "Grave
is the effect that flows out, ever-reddening.
Surrendering. I awake.
The world takes what I make. What I make the world takes."

The day felt as if it had another webbed across it, like
    foam on sand.
To walk into that day was to walk into another. Fine webs or
    strands touched his face. Wind blew the yellow
    shore weeds on the shore
and made constructions. It made a Fatherland
of lotus blue and jade-green waves. Evermore
jade than pacified, it lives in its collages. The sun puts its oar
into the sea, bright sailor, this day webbed with the foam
of another. Could it do more
as it floats up toward the ocean's red bio-novel nights to
    prove it's a strange home?
The night goes into the mountain-tops to roam.

The Curvature of the World

The curvature of the world
is charged with prescience;
so that you might vanish
off the slopes of a snow-freighted
mountain; so that you might reappear
in the shadow of a marble compass
in an esplanade, wearing blue velour.
So that where the future bears
a needle, so be it. And you still
might vanish in your own prescience,
as snow melts off blue slopes
in May-time; you might be pruned
from your very own life.

The Raphael of Cats

Godefroi Mind, Swiss painter, was called
the Raphael of Cats. Optaciana and Plutarca,
two cats of his device, were brought to life
in green and scarlet oils, shimmeringly
stalking cardinals through the grass. Cats
creeping he made, true, but cats pleading
just as well: a detachment of cats well turned out
in frocks to hold vigil before the Purba
Milk Factory, whose high windows Mind has rendered
dim and broken, walls damp and lichen-covered—
never will they lap at blue saucers there.
Do we accuse Mind of anthropomorphism
for his cats at table smoking cheroots and calabash
pipes over games of angel beast and hearts?
For there are striped cats joyous in Apennine meadows,
treed cats, ever-regal, in the topmost boughs,
and cats asleep—dreaming apparently.
But there are also sycophantic cats, who bow
in the courts of parrot kings and seem poised
to execute their green directives—most uncatly.
And can we forgive the painter his beefeater cats
in powdered wigs, or his curious cats,
who await the tolling of an hour
for a mechanized bird to spring from a yellow
clock-face? Can we turn instead to his better work—
his belfry cats who gaze down on the long field grasses
all night long from high, dark places. These are
like queens on an onyx chessboard, sculptural,
nocturnal. His best cats are not cats
that look like people, or even any person's
idea of a cat. They bear little resemblance,
in fact, to cats.

The Cloud

An eyeball-shaped cloud was floating
over the summer houses. You eyeballed it
serenely from the amaranth meadow. Time was
one would take up a syrinx and sing to it.
Now it passes, ghostily, mostly unnoticed
at low altitudes over an Argus-eyed nation.
I bawled at the loss—its obit on newsprint
large as the sky. I, bald as brimstone
brimming with horror. My hazel peepers
were going in a circular orbit, heaven
to earth and back again, scanning that
field between abyss and zenith. There
was, at least, the sun, eyeball-sized,
bright as a diamond hammer. Something
happened. I balled up my fists into gel-filled
orbs, put them up there—no cigar. I kneed
the earth, putting down two scratched patellae
in the dirt beside a maize-bordered pasture
—the basic looking-for-something-I-lost
or asking-for-something posture.

Sleep Thing Militant

I passed by people making
love in the grass, and then I passed
by people in the many gigantic grasses,
who seemed in thrall to a thing outside themselves:
giant strands of green that placed them
two by two beside themselves and one another.
But the grass grew toward a sun they kept
beyond the dewpoints, and they stayed down
and watched the stream, whose water, nickel negative,
grew darker as the grass-points tilted over it.
The people are becoming each other's companions.
The stream is a pencil-thin of darkness
rolling toward the arboretum where the tall
trees grow, chiming and lofting in the gargantuan dark.

And whose copper appurtenance doth radiate
in sunrise, epic sunrise, to lay down
golden stripes upon the green?
And top-heavy humans, elegant in top hats
and alabaster dragon-headed canes like branches
from the crabapple shorn, pass. Copper
sunrise came and in the grass a she-wolf
like a naiad, and in the other grass a she-male,
like a naiad adjourned from the strict arboretum.
Look—the endgame, elegant and cruciform,
the piece of machinery, motorized, that bears
a giant yellow scoop, which it holds aloft, and
holds, holds up and up against the sky.

And then we were driving on a hilly country road
where gently waving cornstalks rose

fifty feet or more into the air, and swayed
in the sky, chiming and lofting, and silver aeroplanes
   with many
divers engines were also in the sky, climbing
in triangular formations, looping and rolling,
and coming back to earthbare earth, and skylark
earth, barely missing our vehicle. It was a sleep thing.
Sleep thing militant. Sleep thing triumphant.

My heart sinks to see the water-sky
and ice-sky, tinted with orange and rose-color
indicative of frozen seas. Because we
were driving and driving away from the trees
and toward a land insane
with innovative birds and premonitions; and colored lights
and gold brocade of grass afire; and planes ascending,
and coming home to malterranic earth
and angry earth, and coming home to sleeping,
peaceful earth. Sleep thing
militant. Sleep thing rampant.

Why the Sleep thing in the sky?
For an ode to a skylark, a battle
is being fought in the sky, lately
on the ground, in the heart. Ode
to the Battle in the Heart.

Cadenza

What is the shield of Faith, and the breast-plate
of Hope, to the fruit of the date palm?
For the fronds are like pellucid ramparts.
And the speal-bones used in divination quiver
on the back of his hand, for the future
quivers thereon like a feather. The sidewinder
shucked off the shroud like a farm-girl earing maize,
like golden-leafed appliqué left on the floor.
And you will apprehend a covert thought, that
somehow in the music's pause comes the cadenza,
in the slab-like silence where it seems no music could survive.
You are called upon to listen for it, and when you hear it,
as you will, it will be yours. Fronds sway in the air
over Comb Jelly City.

Titan Cement

Everyone loves Titan Cement.
The houses half-built, bristling
with steel rods in the sun beating down
on the asphalt will be made whole,
and all will be made whole.
And construction on the airport
is scattered across the horizon
like the rough points of the naked trees,
and Titan Cement will complete
its acrostic, which will spell out
something like a long dark column
and its shadow on the macadam.
It is broad daylight.
It is the whole world and headlessness.
It is broad sunlight, and long,
and past the signs for zinc and black tubes
rush the trucks bearing bags
of Titan Cement to the horizon.
Past the sad brick factory
and black cisterns, Titan Cement
is coming!

Analects

The analects are hidden in the plums
and the plums are spilling from the horn
on the banquet table. What part

of the ceremony is this? A shovel full
of dirt flung against a blue hedge, the tassels
of the golden bantam corn hanging in the sky

like streamers in the sun. We are part
of it, as L is for appLe and A is for boAt.
The green roof of the theater is glazed

with snow-water, like the clang
of a four-sided bell. The very first heartbeat
came from nowhere—so will the last.

Boy Leading a Horse

If you exist; and if, furthermore,
somewhere in the world, this world,
small yellow birds hide in wet leaves,
or other shy, rose-colored, rose-figured
forms; if you once had the power
of being nameless, once, on the day
you were born—then he is looking
straight through you and past these,
and we must, for a moment, agree with
his disdain. You too were once
the tallest thing for miles; you too
were leading or were led through
the imagined and the unimaginable;
you were once this young and fire-new,
you never learned to compromise, like
this earth and sky, and you would never
compromise, like the line that splits
the earth from sky. It is a line
that splits the world in two,
that would sunder your very life
forever. You have felt the sun
and shadows falling on your body.
You have been unspeakably one thing
and unspeakably not and never another;
your world was at war forever.
You too were older and prouder than the sky,
and regarded us this darkly, unblinkingly.
You were something more than human: a boy.
And something powerful walked beside you.
It towers over you still. And it submits
to your control, which you exert with
concentration, with forgetfulness—
with a dark and child-like gesture.

The Mountain

After the demands of the body
have been met; and after the red hay
has been baled and set aside for sunset—

And after having met the demands of
the mind (Mind One and Mind Two)
and the sweet laughing children who divide you—

And you have lost track of what makes
a year, for a few seconds; that is, we pass
through a windowless room where the lesson

has been prepared. That is, a little after
you have extracted sweet lotions from
the red leaves and the green leaves,

I come here, to this place, which is nothing
but a monument of glass, a building
with towers, stairways, courts all glass,

surrounded by the vaginal sea beneath heaven;
and nothing can be read there, no messages
are hidden there, and every new second

for as long as I can remember has seemed
equally late, equally long shadows falling
across the afternoon, the molten light

in the windows of the old mint on the hill
and the new mint on the other hill across
the river. And after

answering what has been demanded
of me, and I am exhausted, and full of doubt
I wake up rested on a sandy lakeshore on a wide

open lake plain, and day is breaking, the sky
a red plate over the water, the reddish water.
And yes, I have my suitcase, which I open

with a small brass key, and find there all
I can take stock of: papers, notes, lists, poems,
rows of opaque colored jars shining with

some liquid. And the air snaps suddenly
with clean, cold wind, and yellow super novel pages
and Chinese hundred dollar bills go snapping into the air,

and some menus and pink flyers and sun-bleached
manifestoes, and the tall yellow grass around me
lays down flat, the sand tossed up, and I

struggle just to close my flapping coat. And when
I turn my back to the wind, and when I finally
open my eyes, I see the mountain

green against the air.

And all the things I've lugged here
go flying in a blizzard toward it.
While I had been asleep,

and stars were circling the sky
though the sky is blue as glory-of-the-snow,
the mountain was behind me.

And while I had been laboring
and frightened, I'd been sleeping
and the mountain was behind me,

tall and blinking with its spruces,
wide awake.

The Superman in Front of the Supermarket

There is a bigwig down on the street.
He is wearing a frightwig, or a powder wig.
And he is wearing a power suit, sun-powered
or wind-powered, perhaps. The fabric glints
and reticulates like an anaconda. I'm unsure
of image verification procedures, but I'd venture
to say "Lay low" is a greeting
that is apropos.
I don't know. His shirt-studs shine
like hope, like yellow soap.
There is a time to ravish and a time to woo.
Have I finished the input of info
regarding this man? The sun
is exploding off his golden shoulders.
His eight-piece suit
is padded with brocade or something.
It makes me feel guilty, or quilty.
Why can't the day last forever?
The man is amazing and twilit as
the shade grows long, and they hasten
to polish the last chrome appurtenances
down there at the car wash. A man
walks by with a dog I could swallow whole.
His choice of companions seems to be
an insult to something—perhaps to the
human spirit. But permit me
to stretch out my wings once more
and sing the praises of our silent
standing man, standing like a challenge
to all our empty movement, silent
like a stern indictment of any sentence

we could utter, shining in grand
spectral tweeds, proud as fire,
as finely whiskered as Zapotec gold,
high as ice-spired Everest, disappearing
slowly in the nimbus clouds.

Great Ones

Great ones are not simply sitting in the age by themselves,
under peach trees, in the rain.
Great ones may have mountain lilies in them, fast asleep.
Great ones may recline on golden sofas, fallen into dead stares,
or sleep on the docks of the black-watered factory basin
late at night. They may form by imperceptible growth,
        like seashells.
The power behind the mountain may say something to
        the great ones,
may say something flattering, and so may the boiling sea,
and so may the sea grass in the salt wind.
Will the setting sun say something to the great ones?
Will they foretell the future, which is near?
The silver arch flashes in the winter sky.
And great ones wade into the Mississippi with the river-boats,
and fish leap up into the hairy arms and hairiness of great ones,
and pelicans stiffen at their suicidal instincts
and put sticks and twigs into the hair of great ones.
They build their structures on the heads of great ones.

Do they fear? Flowers, minor beings, never fear, are never
frightened; and can this be said about the great ones?
Malice will never invade one swan soundlessly.
Leafless trees may joylessly despise you
though they are serene as deep space.
The ocean is craftily solemn.

Yet the mountain, after avalanche, is remorseless. It stands
remorselessly, kinged mountain, winged by cloud-forms.
It never knew the power of being lost.

Great ones were never at home on the earth. They
were never part of the earth. They simply
slept on the earth, and awoke on the earth, overcome.

The Firemen

And what do the firemen dream?
The firemen sleep in bright red mansions,
umber manors in terrific states of tension,
where all day yellow lamps are burning daylight
uselessly above the archways, where the trucks
with curving tusks are sleeping, waiting to be driven
to the buildings miserific by the firemen.
Who at this moment sleep. And huge clouds are soaring
over the buildings and over the fire mansion, and burning
purple clouds are moving out toward the horizon.
And blue terrific clouds are passing over the flags
on the supermarket roof, the flags which become the method
for the wind to ask its questions, and stars are passing over
the dark, round earth.
                              And the people play pinochle
in pinnacles that standeth all aglitter though
in earshot of the Klaxon
as they rush through the truculent streets to reach them.
                              The firemen dream
of a bird with magic wings that comes to show them vengeance.
And it is forming like a cloud above the station,
forming and shaping its deep blue plumage
with the wingspan of a falcon, innocent
and vicious as a falcon.
And the saw-palmettos darken,
their crested head-dresses set asway. And the firemen
come with sunrise, and sunrise comes with a sword
                    and cut-gold,
and sunrise comes with entropy, its weapon.
And sunrise comes with a sword.

The Ball Cube

Who invented the ball cube?
It was a great achievement
of the night, of artificial night.
It came into the world a stranger,
and would be a stranger once again.
The tusks of the water park rose
into the red placidity of night
like the head and shoulders
of a girl named Henna Manggham.
And a small green statue
with a shattered hand
stood beneath the unlit E
of Free State Steel's great logo.
Look: lilac cannon fire lights
the great clock towers
over City Vague Bo-Peep.
And has the ball cube's
great hour passed? Has
chain lightning chimed
in the steeple? It is a new
season, and it seems the ball
cube's time comes round once more,
rolling end over end with a clang,
and a clong.

Abracadabra

The old man flew his pointed kite Abracadabra.
"There is a lesson here," he told the boy,
the amazing boy who had no ears, the boy
who had gills, and a brilliant orange body
pulled up from the sea by the old man.
He made the kite dip down toward the counterpointed
gables, and told the amazing boy, "Look now:
The Searcher uses gravity selfishly, as a point
to prove his argument. But the little birds
of God don't hear him, because they have made
themselves amazing, just like you."
The lackluster waves of the sea grew louder.
How they lusted to see what gravity did to the boy!
And the orange kite floated with joyous abandon
like a boy borne aloft by the waves of the sea.

The Iliad

The mountain's sartorial rain, its
huge lapels, its chapel in a valley,
its purple fleece, its flowers.
The city's orange coat
of light at dawn, its towers
magnified through leaves festooned
with dew and mossy screens, spider webs
and spider wigs. The city and the mountain:
there they stood, one versus the other,
a highway lined with silver poles and cables—
standard-bearer; a river bearing chunks of ice
and balls of mud—ambassador. One would
transform the other. One would annihilate,
charged with trepidation; both were eternal.
And so, under sun, they were a fugue.
One grew inside the other. One resolved
the other's doubt. One's self-hatred
transformed the other under the sky. There are
brilliant green missiles in the sky.
There is a mountain, shy in the rain,
magnificent. There is a city, harmless pylons jacketed in
     brilliances.
Clouds came into the sky, darkly,
bringing peace.

Red Soda

A poisha is one-hundredth of a taka
to the Bangladeshi waiter eating yogurt
on an overturned milk crate. "Dear Dax:
I wish Vishnu could've seen your face
when I came floating down majestically
like some great feather falling from the
roc's intangible plumage—and landed here!
I am tired. Night presses on into a mass
of unearthly gazelles. I remember sleeping
in the shadow of the Okay Soda mill.
Everything devilish was very far away from me.
The huge fan leaves of the cradle tree above me
waved as if to say, 'How beautiful I am.'
And I agreed: How beautiful you are.
The things of this world were not put here
for me to argue with.
The huge blue eye of a tiger mosquito
looking at me like plum wine.
I have a great dream
of being something other than what I am:
The universe is a cone of plenty colors.

I wonder how he handles his awesomely
replenishing children. Even the one
with the freaky green eyes,
and the doll in his arms whose eyes
flick open to reveal its freaky green eyes.
For it is amazing to see the streets at lunch time,
filled with girls and boys in black pants
and white shirts, black skirts and black ties.
The patience of man knows no bounds.

While he dines his table legs are propped
up by copies of the Uganda Monitor
folded thrice. They have no hospitalism,
and even their children dare to say the X-word!
They are minor demons. Yet since before
chess was invented there have been men
with fangs and silvery faces, roaring tigers,
snow tigers, and the worldly strutting by
to touch your every hope; it is nothing
but a loach choking on a katydid.
Man is mortal. Woman is delicate.
The Padma. The Meghna. The Jamuna.
The black god, like the yellow
of an egg, who distributes life among us
as a schoolmaster distributes mangoes among boys;
The Earth, the sun, the moon, the sky,
the water of the Ganges is pure, and I
sharpen the dagger of procrastination
while he pleads with me to come to him,
transformed, transfixed, transfigured.
Golden balls are floating in the sky—
just look at them!"

El Arco Iris Olmec

Talking about the Mayan rapture
rain fell on an ancient civilization
just as it now falls on the green grass
it has abandoned. Many were eating papaya
every morning, just like I was.
Many one's child got lost in the market
and were dozing for hours in vegetables pushed
into pyramid candles and prisms like I was.
The instress eats them away like beowulf.

Then someone buying a papaya rooster.
All frisson in its plumage, all unusable like ghosts.
Fifty thousand wraiths glow orange above the hills
and then a rainbow. Something agave
is revived. The shadow
of a luna moth behind the window.

The Eucalyptus

In the rose mallow west of the Western World, in a city founded
by a soldier and built around a fortress, a fortress cut
from the pine and myrtle, in a city that expanded
like the dreams of the soldiers who perished in the arms
of sleep in Donner Pass and Emigrant Gap, here
the eucalyptus looms, and here the magpies gather
on the wet grass. Oranges blossom and lemons flare,
and the new Rosarian arranges his rose lake roses
that redden on their skeletal stems, here in the center
of California. "Eucharist," the root of which means
"thankfulness," same as the root of the giant trees
whose flesh, or bark, peels down in long green strips,
whose oil washes us clean. "Eucharist," which means
the act of giving solemn thanks, even in the act
of taking, as you might give thanks for a tree that
shades you from the sun, or as you may give thanks
to the sun, who is evergreen, as is the eucalyptus.

The tree is a kind of myrtle. Or a kind of martyr.
An evergreen retains its leaves throughout the seasons;
so do the conifers, holly, and the myrtle. Which includes
our eucalyptus. On this silent night, the eucalyptus
is green, the radiant eucalyptus radiating into green,
though it's winter, and in the snowy hills machines
are trembling in the snow. In the mountains
a young man dies. Another man dies as he leans against
a tree, a ponderosa pine, itself a conifer, an evergreen.
His son writes "help" in the snow, which the wind
keeps covering, and the father is overcome by sleep.
The train, but a zephyr in the mountaintops, is derailed in
    heavy snow,

and the snow keeps falling, covering the tracks,
like a man overcome by sleep. The train, Zephyranthes,
amaryllis, is a shepherdess who sleeps. Our young man
is like a machine trembling in the snow. He is trying
not to sleep. Cold comes in jasper-colored waves.
The nightjar is a nocturnal bird that feeds on moths,
gnats, and beetles. A child dies, a father dies,
but a radiant tree, the eucalyptus, the humble myrtle,
everlastingly is green, green and everlasting is its green.
The conifers stay so under iron plates of ice,
but our radiant eucalyptus stands above them, ringed
in magpies. Even in December it will stay so.
Our magpies flicker, existing, non-existing,
weaving in between the trees. They bring a chattering sound,
their only gift beside their plumage, which is black with
ornamental patches of white.

Magpie, help me see the eucalyptus, which is evergreen.
You are the pathfinder, you who were here when the first
soldiers came, fearful through the snow. The ingredients
of winter are not happy. They are beautiful. A father
overcome by sleep. A train derailed. Or words that the wind
keeps covering. This too is part of a winter night, on the eve
of a birth, a gift beyond all workings of intention.
The magi leave their gifts, which are meant to be received,
not understood. Cold comes in jasper-colored waves,
cold calms and cold covers, and the nightjar comes
down calling. But the myrtle is radiant and green. A train
is lost in the monsters, or lost in the mountains, a man is lost
in the snow in the monsters, but he also has his gratitude,
which is beyond the mountains and the monsters, ultramontane.
And in the faithful it is evergreen. Myrtle means "gratitude."
Martyr means "gratitude," and so do the men in the snow,
the soldiers who volunteered their bodies as kindling
so their comrades could survive. They said, "Take my body,"

when they died. And they were brought, like harvest home,
to the festival of Nine, were greeted by the magpies,
or the magi, following the opalescent Pole Star.

Polaris glittered over Amaryllis as she slept.
It seemed to say, "Some will stay in the fields,
and when the snow comes covering they will stay so."
The pine bears a cone as its fruit, in the ponderosa pine,
a tree of great stature, its crystal cones glitter, like the scales
of the frost-bird, golden plover. It is "eucone" in the winter,
and its crystal cones glitter, and the shimmering cones
of the ponderosa glitter.
I have strayed like a hiker through a white-out
away from my intended destination. Which was
to tell you about the quiet of this evening. I could perhaps
go on forever, despite my intentions, and when I return,
like bringing harvest home, be changed, despite my wishes.
Because what am I to something evergreen, who am
ever-changing? And in my ever-changingness, I look
to the humble myrtle, the radiant eucalyptus, because
I cannot understand what brought this day, which itself
is evergreen. I write these words in the snow, which
the wind may cover, hoping that the morning, that Rosarian,
will bring new birth and peace, a peace beyond my understanding.
And yield to the green of the myrtle tree, and the green
of the pathfinding eucalyptus, radiant above me. And give
them my gratitude. Dedicated on this day, December 25, 1996
to Gina and her daughter, who will be born any day now.

Forest Law

Some corn was planted in the Western World.
A rabbit waited in the grass.
The world would pass, that mastiff, and leave him,
a shivering child called Forest Law, alone
to search for green lucerne where an ichneumon crop
    pernicious slunk
across the fields, sunk into its sockets, and took hold.
"If the demons appear as angels and say the things
    angels would say,
then how would one distinguish what is true?"

The moth bean waits. It doesn't study futurology,
it is still as a child, the child of beautiful people.
Daylight, be its integrand; nightshade be its bliss.
He unexpectedly turns out to be
the lone player of himself.

Forest Law, when the Maker hid you
in the grass; when he woke you; when
your dream was interrupted by the thunder,
the sky stammering, and the grass that kept you
in its unifying green beneath it all divided, pentamerous,
into many parts like argonauts with beautiful names.
When the Maker takes you in the blue reeds
of his deltas, when the Maker makes
the cornstalks flare into braids, threads, and fringes;
when the Maker sets the skeletal horizon
shaking like a rosebud on a rain-splashed stem,
in a rose-bed shining in its red-rose cauldron,
in a rigorous, rising garden in the reddening east:
the world is still what you think it is.

Book Consisting of Seven Poems

The White Saucer

The Black Volta River in Burkina Faso starts on a red
slope, it trickles down a blue stone, it is all friction under
the ever-August sky. I woke up beside it like a flame,
blinking in a tangle of ilex, this day the aggregate of all my
wakings; one fixed-wing craft was looping in the tall sky.

Your dream was a graph of force. Mine meant nothing,
like an octagon handshake.

Hansel and Gretel woke up too, in a stand of aspens on a
bed of blue moss when the midnight sun was a mothering
hand stroking the wet meadow. Yawning, with key money
pinned to silver hoods, they are doomed and priceless! You
are too young to be lying there like burnt matchsticks on
a white saucer that turn to cinders at the slightest touch,
as a flame quivers on a wick in a room far away, as a young
black horse flicks his mane free of lacewings.

In an enormous sleigh bed, much too big for his small
body, the boy awoke again, alone, beside an open window,
where the wind billowed in the grass-green curtains and
turned the foxed pages of the book he had been reading.
And the wind turned the foxed pages as he fell back to
sleep.

Orange Cars

The new V train with its Byzantine
routes and caveats—it seems
like a priggish old collector
who pretends to be humble.
Sure, he is satisfied with "just"
a cup of tea: but a cup of lapsang
souchong spiced with grasses bleached
in Baltic sun, and wild
herbs that once hacked down
writhe gaily on the forest floor
when they feel the light—which is
exactly what we do. We stood
on the corner watching
the beautiful orange vintage cars
drive past, reminding us
with bright curved fenders
that it is always night below ground,
and always almost day above.

The Hero Children

The hero children have been pardoned,
and here they come, striding from the ruins,
raised by wolves. This is the exterior
life of a man: to ever stand and tally
the static count of the Pleiades, to stoop
to pull the okra, go down deep,
and then as if by accident
unearth the purple jar of kim chee,
cabbage ever rotting into acid salt.
The kelp-colored leaves preen,
beetle-bright above the dirt-poor
who plead with some strange intelligence

that preserveth well the roundness of a circle:
"Do not crush the garlic shirt-studs
of the hero children!"

The Sweatshop behind the Sweetshop

Then I slipped, and germs were all over me.
The opal slipped from my watch fob
and rolled forth toward the ditch.
It gleamed like jet, a cygnet rippling
through ice wine.
I washed my hands in the stream,
and read the glass atlas in the waters,
heard the buzzing of electric cutters
cutting aspen branches, and Marden,
co-star of House Despicable, brushing
her long hair, not a Hegelian chocolate
amethyst, not the jacinth adjacencies
that sunlight makes on beige flowers—
O what an accomplishment then, to be
a garden rake rusting joylessly in dewy clover,
that or the last orange doctor burn.
I ran my hand through my dewy clover,
washed it in the sweetwater rolling off fronds,
then I slipped on a spot of milk on the stair
in the building where my men were sifting amaranth
        for lavender.
I fell down the stairs in a lint tuxedo,
down stair to stair to where they kept the yellow
motors running and yellow industrial filth, down
to where bare light bulbs, burning daylight,
lit labor, one's Machiavellian brainchild brought to light
and, once launched, offshored, outsourced, drained
and strapped for rupees.

Bel and the Dragon

And in the town in the valley
the sun dripped acid on the brass
adown in the square before the courthouse.

Mr. Linus Nonsmoker leaned
against a Norway maple,
red leaves against the cold air
and bliss, surveyed the fire-pink
buildings in the valley below.

Another fellow, in a fire-colored
jumpsuit, was sitting in full lotus
on the tip of a dandelion
wondering what to do next.

Just as no triangle stands
sans the lumber of its standing, minus
the sunny place in the woods
where gentry felled the aspen,
so you become blameless.
Such light clutched the throat
of the brass statue, such strangeness.
A bell tolled over the obelisk, perforce
something clanged in the emptiness inside itself,
it named itself, and named itself again,
and when it reached the twelfth telling
found its essence.

Quiet Leaves

He asked the book what it meant.
The book did not oblige.
The book just kept repeating itself.
He closed the book. So the book
sat there on the dark mahogany, silently.
Its leaves were quiet leaves.
The book would not be argued with.
Day broke like a white grenade.
Catamarans were passing under bridges
footloose under the sun, silver
honorifics blazing on their sails.
The book maintained its stodgy silence,
total and tyrannical. A stack
of yellow newspapers smoldered into obsolescence
on a windowsill. The telephone directory
seemed to be shedding its wrinkled skin.
The reader looked out at the white
boats, and continued his fruitless match
of wills against the quiet leaves.
Here is the emblem of the book: Thee, reader.

The Book with the Perfect Ending

Oxen plough from left to right
and back again, like someone with
a writing problem, but perfect
in their own way, in the way
of oxen ploughing. The sharecropper
does create a matrix, does procreate;
his ruse smolders deep beneath the earth.
Maybe it's getting late. The yokel

needs a brickbat for the magpies,
in the poverty of scratched-out
fields—but the farmer wrote
the perfect book with a perfect ending,
the book that ended with a wedding,
where the May King was the groom—
Mogul of the apples and the wildflowers.

What Is To Be Done?

Some poets can't seem to penetrate
and draw meaning from the things around them.
So what was poetry meant to be in the first place?
In the second place, how do you go about it?
To think on this makes my two lobes feel
like two raw hams. It is beyond me. Words
keep chasing around like elves in the fastafazool
or dust rags in the wind; and each
must go about it all, harmonica, melodica,
as if they know not what they do, and how
they do it. You can't write in the green
ink of the trees—I have a mind-block.
We're left with the last thing poetry ever
had. All its weight lies there now. What
it was supposed to do—something else
does that now. Now we meet the Answerer
on his own ground.

Ferdinand the Rail

Poetry is not a mirror, gentlemen, life is not
a cube-version of a mirror, it is
not an expansion of yourself as seen

from outside by all onlookers, including
you. It disappears, gentle man,
from your own sight as you move away,

But it goes on, and the image it reflects
is glazed by the formless ball of each moment,
like sun in the rain. Gentlemen,

you are asleep. And you are there. And beside you
a cold stream is rushing along toward Battersea.
You can't believe your own eyes

most of the time. You barely know yourself.
At times you stand in front of yourself,
boldly: there is an image, like dark bluffs

against the night sky. Light seems to shine out
at you at others, in plangent bolts,
from what was just a formless ball.

Then you step away, you gentle man, you disappear;
you can just see the image of the hallway
leading to an open door, and dappled

shadows. Then you move further away,
and turn around: you are no longer
looking at an image of the world,

or of yourself in it. You are not sure
if you're alive. You can hear cold water
crashing over stones. Your life

is a great transparency.

Lipton Yellow Label Tea

Once I pulled a mask from a bunch
of yellow hay, then closed the box and nailed
it up with a ball-peen hammer—just like nothing
ever happened. It had geometric facial features,
organic knots and a distressed finish
like a fake antique tripod: it appeared
to have been carved from a single teak salad bowl.
I have filled my abode with such "found objects,"
wares from Burkina Faso that fell off the truck,
poly-resin cutting boards, dolls, knives,
a crate of yellowing paper novels by one Agatha
Sideburn, silver cans of bird-nest soda, a grass-green
box of Chinese staples—I extracted a sitar from gruel
and had to peel the mahogany veneer off a goblin
with rusted needle-nosed pliers, and its green
paint flaked off like a brontotherium's single
woodsy tusk, or an apple, all redsy, bobbing
on the Tiber.
I was shipping a whole load of pink ceramic birds
on wicker mats brought from Indonesia
on a rusted-out hulk boat before dawn.
I loaded the pallets onto my truck, and the foreman
came over looking sawed-off and presidential
to harangue me. Blue rats like water-bison
swam up past the pier.

The estuary in the morning is a beautiful idea.
But it has these…how can I put it? Huge blue
refineries, freighters dropping chains, and similar
ghost manifestations. It's haunted by an eighty-
yard-long used condom, lurking around down there

touching the bottoms of the boats, rubbing
along the green-stained keels, infecting them.
Few people have seen it, but I have.
Sorry, I spilled eucalyptus cream
all over the chart—guess I'm not the *cordero
de dios*. There's erica grass crawling over the blue
hoops, too. Anyway, a star flag has been raised. It flung
porn on the world, for the world wants the Ganges
aflood with crystal azaleas, then to have a snowcrab
rise up from its waters. Well, look at it this way.
Dragons fear doves, and doves delight in the trees.
Trees border yam fields in the twilight,
and the Brown Front Love truck idles outside,
the city rising up behind it like a huge switchboard.
From here the sky could govern the plague.
Have you seen the conning tower of a submarine
slowly rise from the Atlantic's cold basalt waters?
With water pouring off its back, it takes a steely aim.
A goggle-eyed man suggested I stay at his Etruscan villa
but I doubted the veracity of his claims that I
would receive the gift of second sight thereafter,
and there like a peregrine falcon waiting on a column
waited I, while the mottled purple sky made arrangements
for its clouds to become the puppets of my will.
Well, I have waited and been, apparently, denied.
I have been given hints as to the wisdom of waiting
while an object of desire is withheld. I have
argued with that wisdom, taken, what's more,
what was purposefully left defenseless and destroyed it,
burned a field before it ripened. O sure,
I am enchanted by the falcon-gentle coming down
through trees, the leafless trees, or a manta ray rising
in a cloud of blood-red silt from the sea floor.
That's Eva, in her apple gown, her vestal
gear and pageantry, and then there is the manufactory

within the mother, primagravida as springtime always
is. But it's a mother insane with love,
is hissing in the giant leaves
in the garden in Anuradhapura.
The willowy motion of the fins on the fish
in the tanks in the Chinese restaurant's window
recalls the monster battles of the past.
Like a huge radish growing in the water cooler,
the wind sweeps down dispassionately.
In a word, it seems to me, the tide has gone out.

In the belling the cat fable
natural juices were flowing under Jersey.
Rain and wet leaves clogged the birdbath.
But the shadow bands rush swiftly across the landscape,
and rose birds and pink birds too.
And the shade-grown tobacco turns golden
as the sky marshal leans back in the moist leaves
to play the grass saxophone. The rabbit-eared
armadillo and the sheep-dog lie down side by side,
the shaggy-mane mushroom and the spider
lie down side by side, caring little, this moment,
for their places on the food web. For by the black,
biting humor, who is bit? After all we've been through
night yet comes on peacefully, forgetfully,
and brews into a bright red liquor.

Peloponnesian Wars

We dream according to what we are.
The infant searching with closed eyes
and open mouth in sleep dreams
of the breast. We don't fault
the newborn for the way she blindly gropes
through space to find the mother
who is sitting in a blue chair
by a window in another room.
A gong has been sounded. The flashing
ebb and flow of life outside
rises like an empty summons.
We have been summoned by something
in a dream, or we have been reaching.
We have been surmounted.
Harsh voices and spread plumage,
Peloponnesian wars, and a sky filled
with water birds struggling
to organize into a V
that will take them home for the winter.
But they don't know yet why they struggle.

The Red Pebble

The sun found the red pebble
in the green grass. It was a coming
together, of sorts, that lasted
an instant, spotless, an instant
of flaring red from green that purged
itself of meaning, of potential
to be any other than
the green Zealot of Red, willingly
neutral, and naked with the praise
of being looked upon.
It's astonishingly round,
and bright, this thing
that no one has seen, that doesn't
exist, this poem's invention,
far from the slanted mineral banks
pale yellow by the river, holding
and withholding,
the reddest possible red,
presently slated for extinction
as the shadow of the larkspur
moves with great poise toward it.

The Prologue

The gargantuan page hovered over the valley.
It was page 5.
And page 5 hung over the castle, like sheets, like clouds,
like…like wings.
Wheat waved in the valley, corn billowed on the slopes,
green…green.
All were lying in the gentle purple shadow of the
Prologue.
It was a story about waves of purple martins flying down
to eat the apple cores.

The Bright Day

We are here today, and today
this world is suddenly ours.
It is sunny in a green meadow, we
are in each other's arms, and behind us
light blue mountains going on forever
under an ancient blue sky; and before us
the day, the blue-green steeples of the sea;
it is ours for a day. Beyond the mountains
the wind is in the flags of a city whose domes,
water-pinnacles, and towers lie spread beneath
the mountain-shadow for some hours in the dawn,
then dazzlingly awaken: they are clean
and new again. We have been here looking
at the sun and listening to the sound of waves
forever. We have also been making a
new-found peace with each other, preparing
a dwelling place. There are bright red markers
in the trees, so startling, and the hours like drops
of water falling off a branch. We are somehow
the consequence of what we have always been.

Crossing the Tappan Zee Bridge

You can see us from so far away.
You can see us, near as silver in the sun,
and nearer. You can see us, blind with joy
and seeing everything around us,
this bridge poised in the dazzling sun
like scissors, and we hold one another's
lives in our hands, like scissors.
I believe the city, not yet visible, exists.
And I believe the city unbelievable
exists—we are racing past the salt trucks,
beneath the green masts
of the sky—we are aloft
between land-forms and their shadows, we
are nowhere. And now
you can see the white buildings
coming through the haze. They
can be seen from miles away, like
a cloud. But the Great Wall
can be seen from space: we all
can be seen from space.

Geoffrey Nutter was born in Sacramento, California. His first book, *A Summer Evening,* won the 2001 Colorado Prize (Center for Literary Publishing, 2001). His poems have appeared in many journals and anthologies, including *The Best American Poetry 1997* and *The Iowa Anthology of New American Poetries.* He lives in Manhattan with his wife, daughter and son.